# GUIDE TO
# ÁVILA

Text, photographs, design, lay-out and printing
completely created by the technical department of
**EDITORIAL FISA ESCUDO DE ORO S.A.**

 ESCUDO DE ORO

## INTRODUCTION

Apart from the outstanding monumental attractions of the city of Ávila itself, the entire province offers the visitor an incredible mosaic of natural landscapes, as well as many fine examples of popular architectural styles, monuments reminding us of the long, rich history of these lands, fascinating folklore and excellent food and drink. This guide proposes five routes enabling the reader to discover this magnificent province. The first is devoted to Ávila, the capital. The second contains a description of La Moraña county in the north, with the towns of Arévalo and Madrigal de las Altas Torres. Next, the third and fourth routes take us to the Tiétar Valley, with Arenas de San Pedro, and the Tormes Valley, where we can visit Barco de Ávila and Piedrahita. On the fifth route, to the Alberche Valley, we can stop off at Las Navas del Marqués and Burgohondo. Finally, this introductory chapter also contains summaries of the local geography and climate, history, festivities and food and drink.

*Amblés Valley. Solosancho: bridge over the River Adaja.*

### Geography and climate

Ávila province, which forms part of the Autonomous Community of Castilla y León, occupies an area of 8,050 square kilometres and has a population of 160,700, of whom nearly 59,000 live in the capital. The

*Ávila at sunset. In the foreground, the Calvary of Cuatro Postes.*

province borders on Valladolid and Segovia provinces to the north and northeast, Salamanca to the northwest, Toledo and Madrid to the south and southeast, and Cáceres to the southwest.

Geographically, the province is formed by a series of mountains and plains protected and articulated by the Sierra de Gredos. Through these mountains run three rich, fertile valleys, each with its own distinctive landscape, so much so that they might be different worlds. To the north lie the Tormes and Alberche river valleys, whilst to the

*Sierra de Gredos.*

*Ávila: West side of the city walls, and the River Adaja.*

south is the light-filled Tiétar Valley. Travelling northwards, we note the stark contrast between these rocky mountain peaks and the plains of Madrigal and Arévalo. The towns here, dotted along the moun-

*Village of Ulaca: Verraco sculpture.*

tain slopes, bestriding rivers or standing amid the vast, solitary plain, still conserve the firm, pure essence of the Castilian character. The province has an extremely cold continental climate, though with notable variations, such as the climate of the Tiétar Valley, where temperatures rarely fall below zero. The same is true of rainfall, which ranges from 1,600 mm in the Sierra de Gredos to 600 mm in the Sierra de la Paramera. Similar contrasts are found, too, in the vegetation, where we pass from oak, chestnut and pine forests, to mountain pasture and scrubland, to the flat northern lands, where practically no trees grow.

## Brief historical summary

Ávila is the land of the Vettons, a Celtic people who settled between the Duero and Tagus rivers in around the 6th century BC, principally in what are now the provinces of

Salamanca, Cáceres, Ávila and Toledo. The surviving legacy of this civilisation takes the form of so-called *verracos*, roughly-carved sculptures of animals resembling at times a bull, at others a wild boar, and which are found all over Ávila province. The next people to settle here were the Romans. *Avela*, the present Ávila, was the main town in this part of Roman Lusitania. After the fall of the Roman Empire, the province was occupied successively by different civilisations: Christians, then Moors in the 8th century, Christian once more after Alfonso III took Ávila in 864, only for it to fall into Islamic hands again until, in 1085, King Alfonso VI of Castile and León finally conquered the territory. Alfonso VI then went on to lay the foundations for growing prosperity at all levels. This period, when the city walls were built, also marks the beginning of Ávila's so-called knightly saga. An army was mustered, comprising hundreds of knights whose main task was to defend the region from attack. However, this army also took part in victorious campaigns against Moorish forces in other places. In 1492, with the Christian conquest of the Iberian Peninsula from the Moors com-

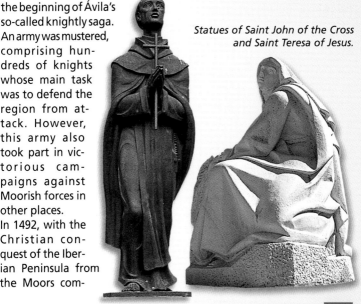

*Mombeltrán: Roman road.*

plete, Ávila entered a period of decadence and decline that lasted until the 16th century, when the wool industry and the religious and cultural works carried out by St Teresa of Jesus and St John of the Cross combined to help shake the province out of its doldrums. In the early 17th-century, however the transfer of the court to Madrid, which led many nobles to leave Ávila, and the ex-

*Statues of Saint John of the Cross and Saint Teresa of Jesus.*

*Avila during the festival of Santa Teresa.*

pulsion of the *Moriscos*, Moors converted to Christianity, on whom the local trade and craft industries depended, plunged the city and surrounding area into lethargy once more. Finally, the arrival of the railway in 1860 and the flourishing of the local service sector and the establishment of new industries in the 20th century enabled Ávila to become one of the most prosperous

*Easter Week.*

provinces in Castilla y León once more, whilst agriculture continued, as ever, to be a leading source of income in the local economy.

## Festivities and folklore

The principal religious festivities here include, particularly, Easter Week in Ávila, catalogued as an event of national tourist interest, as well as *romerías*, religious processions, such as those of El Cristo de la Luz, in Lanzahíta; San Pedro de Alcántara, in Arenas de San Pedro; Nuestra Señora de la Chilla, in Candeleda, and Nuestra Señora de Sonsoles, patron saint of Ávila, in Valle de Amblés. Another important religious celebration is «El Vítor a San Pedro Bautista», which takes place in San Esteban del Valle on February 5 and 11 and July 7 and 18. These events feature magnificent mounted processions, during which young riders declaim «ví-

*Virgin of Sonsoles.*

*Typical costumes.*

tores» or laudatory verses, transmitted orally from father to son. Moreover, the celebrations in honour of the local patron saints in towns and villages all over the province provide excellent opportunities to taste the local cuisine and admire the typical costumes and dances. For women, the local costume consists of brightly-coloured shawls, adorned with patterns and flowers, worn with elegant sashes, whilst the men don short breeches, cloth coats and *polainas,* woollen stockings.

The Carnival is the most attractive of the profane festivities in the province, and is celebrated particularly intensely in Ávila, El Tiemblo, Piedralaves, Cebreros and Arévalo. Other interesting events include, in Ávila in June, «La Ronda de las Leyendas», a programme of activities in which actors recreate legendary episodes from local history at different points in the city, and the Medieval Festival, which takes place in September. Also interesting in Piedrahita each June, are the «Jornadas Goyescas», another season of historic recreations, and the Horse Fair in August.

Amongst the local arts and crafts, the most characteristic articles include particularly hats made from rye straw, still widely used for pro-

*Typical straw hats.*

*Typical gastronomic products.*
*«Las Murallas» Restaurant, Ávila.*

tection against the hot sun. The more elaborate are usually adorned with small mirrors and hearts.

## Food and drink

The cuisine of Ávila is simple, its secrets based above all on the quality of the local produce and a varied range of ingredients thanks to the geographic and climatic variety in the province. To summarise this cuisine, we propose the following menu, full and varied. As an appetizer, particularly in the capital itself, we recommend the typical tapas. The most popular of these are different types of pork sausages, tripe and a potato dish known as *patatas revolconas*

*«Patatas revolconas» and roast suckling pig.*

*Baked trout.*

*Peaches from Burgohondo.*

(boiled, mashed and spiced with paprika and *torreznos*, bacon). For the first course, beans from El Barco de Ávila, *cocido moragueño* stew, or any of the many fine local vegetables dishes. For the main course, roast, fried or grilled meat is always a good choice: roast suckling pig, kid, partridge stew or Ávila beef (from Avileña cattle) can be found on most restaurant menus. Those preferring fish should try trout from the Alberche or Tormes rivers, which enjoy richly merited fame. And to wash down all these fine foods, we recommend wines from Cebreros and El Tiemblo. Finally, diners can choose from amongst a huge range of desserts: the popular *yemas de Santa Teresa*, *huesillos fritos*, *glorias de Ávila* or delicious peaches from Burgohondo.

*«Yemas de Santa Teresa».*

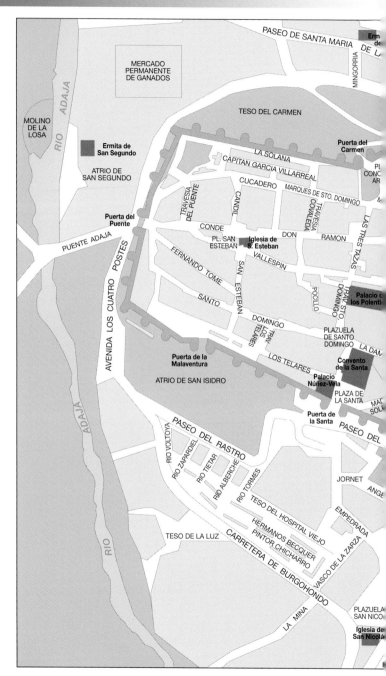

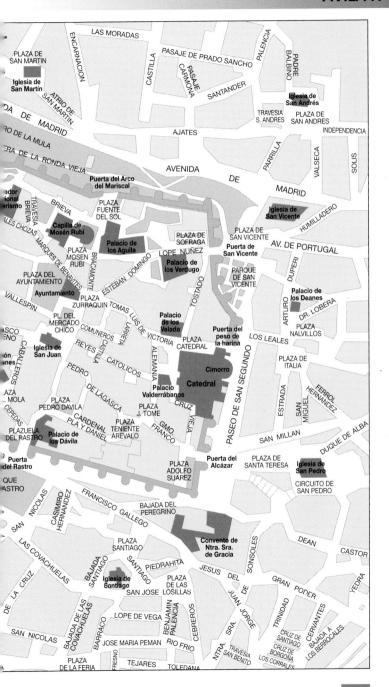

*Aerial view of Ávila.*

## 1. ÁVILA

City walls – Church of San Vicente – Monastery of La Encarnación – Cathedral – Noble houses – Convent of La Santa – Royal Monastery of Santo Tomás – Chapel of San Segundo – Palace of Los Deanes / Avila Provincial Museum – Mystic Interpretation Centre – main squares – St. Teresa of Jesus

Ávila, capital of the province of the same name, lies on a hill overlooking the Adaja River, appearing to the approaching visitor as a huge fortress defended by impressive walls. The city lies at an altitude of over eleven hundred metres above sea level, making it the highest in Spain. In the background, dominating the landscape, soar haughtily the peaks of the Sierra de Gredos, before which extends the Amblés Valley.

The city stands on the site of a Celtiberian settlement populated by the Veton tribe and which, according to Ptolemy, was located in the western extreme of Lusitania and was known originally as Obila. Evidence of these historic origins is found in the numerous verracos, or sculptures of bulls and pigs which decorate the streets and parks of the city. The most famous is the group of four verracos forming «Los Toros de Guisando».

Ávila was christianised in the 1st century AD thanks to the arrival here of Saint Segundo, one of the seven Male Apostles sent by Saint Peter to evangelise Hispania. After the Moorish invasion in the late-11th century the city became part of Castile due to the conquering zeal of Alphonse X, the Wise. From the first moment, this region was occupied by knights from Burgos, León, Asturias and Galicia who, under the orders of Count Raimundo de Borgoña, made Ávila their most important bastion.

This Castilian pride was demonstrated in all its strength and vigour during the uprising of the *Comuneros* at the beginning of the 16th century, in which the city fought for its freedom against the centralist policies of Emperor Charles V. It was during the same century that the Carmelite Order was reformed by Saint Teresa of Jesus, and Ávila lived under the influence of «la Santa», as she was known here, visitors to the city observing the evidence of this at every turn, in every church and convent, continually seeing relics of the saint and hearing her legend told and retold.

But Ávila is also the «Ciudad de los Caballeros» –the city of the knights– and is replete with noble palaces and lordly mansions over whose doors are proud coats of arms and escutcheons. UNESCO added Ávila to the World Heritage list in 1985.

*Statue of a «verraco», boar, in Plaza de Adolfo Suárez.*

*West flank of the walls.*

## City walls

This impressive monument, one of the oldest and best conserved in Spain, is the symbol by which Ávila has always been known. Their construction began in the 11th century, under the orders of Count Raimundo de Borgoña, son-in-law of Alphonse VI. The titanic work was directed by Casandro Colonio and Florín de Pituerga in collaboration with other Spanish architects and with a workforce of 800 men, and was finally completed in 1101.

Building began with eastern side, as this was where the cities was most unprotected, using stone from previous constructions, particularly the old Roman walls, for the most part. However, when these materials ran out the quality of the construction was not adversely affected and as we work our way around to the north we see that the different stretches blend together, reaching the technical quality of the «Cimorro» tower. The initial work-rate could not be maintained for the rest of the walls, however, and the size of the ashlar used decreases gradually, then becomes mixed with brick and rough stone, the distance between towers becomes greater. The walls are three metres thick and 12 high on average, topped

*The apse at the Cathedral known as the «Cimorro».*

*Paseo del Rastro.*

by parapets and lookout towers. The most original feature are the semicircular towers built every 20 metres, whereas other similar walls have bastioned towers.

*Ávila's city walls.*

*The city's walls can be visited at the top. The open route is 1,700 meters long and it can be started at different points.*

The city walls are also perforated by various gates, the most important of which are found on the east side. These are the **Puerta de San Vicente** and the **Puerta del Alcázar,** which are protected by two huge twenty-metre high towers joined at the top by a semicircular arch. None of the other gates match this spectacular monumental quality.

*The Alcázar Gate and the monument to Saint Teresa of Jesus.*

*The San Vicente Gate.*

*Puerta del Puente, or Bridge's Gate.*

*The Malaventura Gate.*

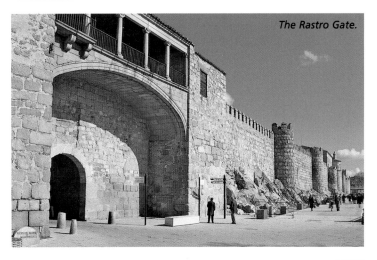

*The Rastro Gate.*

Gate of the Saint.

Gate of Peso de la Harina.

Ávila covered with snow.

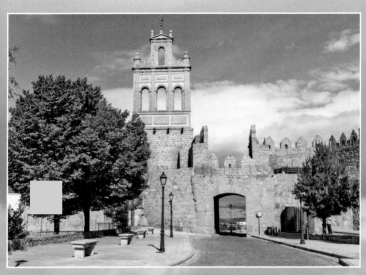

*The Carmen Gate.*

*Church of San Vicente.*

## Church of San Vicente

Having admired the walls, our tour of the city can begin with this church, a fine building con-

*Church of San Vicente: detail of the portal in the main façade.*

structed in the mid-12th century in honour of saints Vincent, Sabina and Cristeta, siblings who suffered martyrdom on this site in the 4th century.

The building, in the shape of a Latin cross with nave and two aisles, was constructed in two stages: in the first, Romanesque, phase, the apses, the crypt («Soterraña») and the walls up to the cornices were completed, whilst in the second late –12th to early-13th centuries, and proto-Gothic in style, therefore–, the vaults were covered and the elegant portals decorated with an iconographic design. Though the works can be considered complete from that date, the present dome (not as heavy as the original) was built during the 14th and 15th centuries, the towers

*The nave of the church of San Vicente.*

were crowned and the sacristy was terminated, as were other elements. Inside is the **Cenotaph of Saints Vincent, Sabina and Cristeta,** which also dates back to the early-13th century. The most interesting feature are the sides, depicting the martyrdom and death of these Spanish saints on 27 October 306.

*Tomb of the Holy Martyrs.*

The apses of the church also contain interesting baroque altars, and the **Tomb of San Pedro del Barco** (1610), commemorating a famous local hermit on whose death, to avoid argument about his final resting-place, his remains were placed on the back of a mule, its eyes bandaged, which brought the saint to this site.

**Monastery of La Encarnación**

We now take Avenida de Madrid to Paseo de Santa María de la Cabeza, at the end of which is the **Church of San Martín,** dating back to the early 18th century and featuring a beautiful

*"The Embrace", by García del Barco (15th century).*

*Romanesque carving representing one of Saint Vincent's sisters.*

*Monastery of La Encarnación.*

*Church at the Monastery of La Encarnación.*

15th-century Mudéjar tower, the proudest in the entire city and Calle de Cardeñosa, passing through the popular district of Ajates (populated by the workers who built the city walls) then leads as to the **Monastery of La Encarnación**.

This institution was founded in 1479 as a *beatería* (a house where communities of lay sisters live) in a former synagogue converted into a church and donated to this end by Cardinal Fonseca. In 1515, it was converted into a Carmelite convent and dedicated to the Incarnation of Our Lord. Its importance lies in the fact that it was here that Saint Teresa of Jesus remained for 27 years as a simple nun and three as prioress.

Few original elements remain here, apart from the front, with its Gothic-style semicircular arch of enormous voussoirs. The interior dates back to the 17th century, as does the beautiful

*Cathedral: main façade.*

*Entrance at the south façade.*

baroque decoration. The cell of Saint Teresa of Jesus has now been transformed into a wide chapel containing the original elements, rediscovered during restoration in 1968, when remains of the kitchen were also found.

The museum is important to help us to understand what the Reformation of the Order of Carmel meant, returning it to its former rigour, mitigated by Pope Eugenius IV in 1432.

## Cathedral

Now, taking Calle de Mosén Rubí, leaving on the right the **Casa de los Verdugo,** another example of Renaissance civil architecture, we reach the rear section of the **Puerta de San Vicente,** continuing to the Cathedral.

**Ávila Cathedral,** which was begun in the late-12th century, is the work of the legendary *Maestro* Fruchel. Its Gothic vaults were commenced at the head, which rises over the city walls in the so-called «Cimorro» tower and which was completed in 1211. The rest of the building was not finished until the late-14th century, thanks to the efforts of Bishop Sancho de Ávila.

The exterior features two fronts, the oldest of them, on one side, known as that of the Apostles (13th century).

The cathedral has a nave and two aisles with a large transept and head with ambulatory. The material used in its construction is sandstone speckled with ferrous red stains which, although attractive to the eye, is very fragile, and is therefore mixed with granite.

Inside is the **choir,** a Renaissance-style work dating from the second third of the 16th century and decorated by sculptures by Juan

*Ambulatory.*

Rodríguez and Lucas Giraldo depicting scenes from the childhood of Jesus. Inside are magnificent stalls by Cornielis of Hol-

*The choir.*

*Altarpiece of the High Altar.*

*Nave of the Cathedral.* ▶

land, assisted by Rodríguez and Giraldo as well as Isidro Villoldo. The **High Altar,** three times higher than it is wide, is a work of tremendous architectural daring. It is decorated with a splendid altarpiece admirably combining painting with sculpture. This is a Gothic work commenced in 1499 by an anonymous artist and continued from 1508 by the sculptor Vasco de la Zarza. Pedro Berruguete was commissioned with the paintings, but he had only completed *The Prayer in the Garden* and *The Flagellation* by the time of his death. His work was therefore continued by the *Maestro* Santacruz with *The Adoration of the Magi, The Crucifixion* and *The Resurrection.* The series was then completed by Juan de Borgoña.

The next great work is the magnificent **sepulchre of «El Tostado»,** situated at the rear of the high altar, in the ambulatory. This masterpiece of Spanish Renaissance art is by Vasco de la Zarza and represents Alonso de Madrigal, «El Tostado» (the swarthy), bishop of Ávila.

Most interesting of the remaining **chapels** are that of San Juan,

Sepulcre of "El Tostado".

Altar of San Segundo.

with two good Gothic tombs: the Chapel of Nuestra Señora de Gracia, containing the tomb of Sancho Dávila, the bishop under whom work began on the cathedral; the Chapel of San Antolín, with an interesting Renaissance altarpiece; and the Chapel of San Segundo, founded in 1595, designed by Francisco de Mora and one of whose chaplains was Lope de Vega.

Finally, the **Museum** (founded by the Chapter) is in the Chapel of El Sagrado Corazón and adjoining rooms formerly used as the chapterhouse and archives. Exhibited are excellent collections

Chapel of San Bernabé.

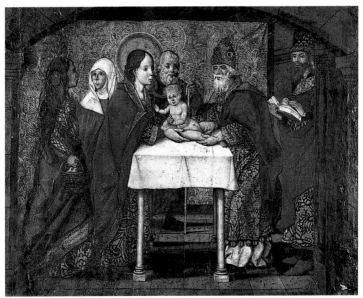

*Triptych of St. Peter (attributed to Fernando Gallego, 15th century, Chapel of St. Peter), and «The Purification» (15th century, Cathedral Museum).*

of sculpture, painting and fine metalwork. The most important work is the great silver monstrance by Juan de Arfe, 1.70 metres high.

## Noble houses

On our route from the cathedral to the Convent of Saint Teresa, we shall now pass by many civil constructions of great in-

*Palace of Los Velada.*

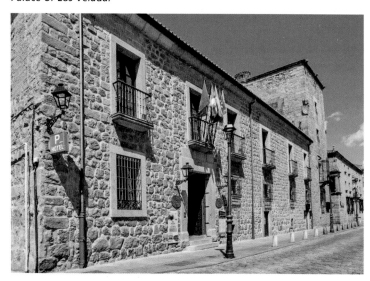

*Palace of Los Dávila: main façade.*

terest. In Plaza de la Catedral itself, we find the following: **Palacio Viejo or Palacio del Rey Niño,** former bishop's residence constructed in the late-12th century, with a front dating to the early-16th, and **Palace of Los Velada,** its main feature being its sharp-cornered tower, without minarets.

Calle de Alemania takes us to Plaza de Pedro Dávila (formerly Plaza de la Fruta), where we find the **Palace of Los Dávila.** Formed by four buildings from different periods, this palace is considered one of Avila's finest medieval sites. The oldest building here, adjoining the Rastro Door, is believed to go back to the 13th century, whilst the other three were built between the 14th and 16th. The robust masonry walls the presence of powerful machicolations and battlements illustrate the eminently defensive design of the building, which adjoins the city walls to the south. The various doors in the palace, all with large voussoirs, are of outstanding interest.

Finally, we take Calle de los Cepedas to Plaza Corral de las Campanas to find the **Tower of Los Guzmanes,** a 16th-century palace where King Alphonse XII stayed when he visited the city in 1878. The **Vettonia Interpretation Centre,** housed in the old palace stables, gives visitors the

*Tower of Los Guzmanes.*

*The Convent of Saint Teresa.*

*Church of the Convent of Saint Teresa.*

*Stained-glass window.*

chance to learn about the culture of the first settlers in these lands.

## Convent of Saint Teresa

This building stands on the site of the house where Teresa was born on 28 March 1515. The convent was founded in 1636 through the munificence of the Count-Duke of Olivares, its patron. The only original element surviving is the place the saint

*Image of Saint Teresa.* ▶

was born, now converted into a chapel.

The **Museum of Saint Teresa**, devoted to the life and works of Ávila's most universal daughter, is installed in the convent crypt.

## Royal Monastery of Santo Tomás

We now take the **Puerta de la Santa,** formerly known as that of Montenegro, through the city wall, taking Paseo del Rastro to

*Convent of Nuestra Señora de Gracia.*

*Church of Santiago.*

*Royal Monastery of Santo Tomás.*

this convent. Firstly, though, we will pause before the **Convent of Nuestra Señora de Gracia,** a late-16th-century work containing a high altarpiece attributed to the sculptors Giraldo and Rodríguez. Another nearby church is that of **Santiago,** which dates back to the early-16th century and features a beautiful octagonal-shaped tower thought to date back to the 14th century because of the marks on the stone and the type of cornice used.

The **Royal Monastery of Santo Tomás** was founded on 11 April 1482 by Doña María Dávila and Fray Tomás de Torquemada in accordance with the last will and testimony of Hernán Núñez Arnalte, treasurer and secretary to the Catholic Monarchs.

The convent is entered through a simple doorway with lowered vault featuring ten granite sculptures by Martín de Solórzano.

Inside, an unusual feature is the fact that the **Presbytery** and the **High Altar** are raised to be almost on a level with the choir, without direct communication with the church, allowing both monks and faithful to follow the mass without disturbing one another. The works of art contained here include the magnificent **Sepulchre of Prince John** (died Salamanca 4 October 1497) in Car-

*Church of the Monastery of Santo Tomás.*

*Royal Monastery of Santo Tomás: tomb of Prince John.*

rara marble, the work of Florentino Domenico Fancelli. The second masterpiece here is the altarpiece over the high altar, decorated with paintings by Pedro Berruguete illustrating the life of Saint Thomas Aquinas. The bench features life-size portraits of saints *John the Evangelist, Matthew, Hieronymus* and *Augustine,* works of great naturalism and rigour, besides a surprising colourfulness.

The **choir** is adorned with fine stalls attributed to Martín Sánchez and dated to around 1492.

*Museum of Oriental Art: Japanese jar.*

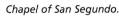

The convent dependencies are distributed around three courtyards, that of the «Noviciado», which lies at the heart of the foundation, surrounded as it is by the principal dependencies, that of the «Silencio» and the «Patio de los Reyes», the former royal residence. One side of this last is occupied by the **Museum of Oriental Art.**

This museum contains the works gathered together by the Dominican fathers in their missions to the Far East, exhibited here since 1964.

## Chapel of San Segundo

This 12th-century Romanesque chapel, particularly beloved of the local people, houses the mortal remains of Saint Secundus, disciple of the Apostle James and first bishop of the city. The chapel or hermitage, which stands on the banks of the River Adaja, near the Puerta del Puente (Bridge Gate), is a simple structure with three apses, slightly inclined, wooden roof and spire. The most interest-

*Chapel of San Segundo.*

*Palace of Los Deanes.*

ing element in it is the tomb of Saint Secundus, finely carved in alabaster by Juan de Juni in 1573.

## Palace of Los Deanes / Ávila Provincial Museum

Standing outside the city walls, in Plaza de Nalvillos, this is a 16th-century two-storey building that was once the residence of the cathedral deans and now houses Ávila Provincial Museum. The museum rooms lead off the porticoed courtyard, forming an illustrated history of Ávila and surrounding area from prehistoric times to our days. The museum collections are divided into three sections: archaeology, popular art and fine art.

## Mystic Interpretation Centre

This unusual building, opened in 2004, stands opposite the birthplace of St Teresa of Ávila, in Paseo del Rastro. The centre, unique in Europe, was set up to introduce visitors to the phenomenon of mysticism. Here are mystic texts from all periods and cultures, as well as objects and different materials, illustrating the symbolism attached to them: from stone, sand, concrete, white wax and oxidized iron to Sparta grass and methacrylate. The displays are enriched by the application of lighting and modern technology.

We now complete our visit to the city by returning to the walls along Paseo del Rastro to Plaza de Santa Teresa de Jesús, pausing to admire the **Church of San Pedro,** built during the transition from Romanesque to Gothic, with an attractive front in reddish stone.

*Mystic Interpretation Centre.*

*Church of San Pedro, in Plaza de Santa Teresa or «El Mercado Grande».*

## Squares

Everyday life in Avila revolves around two squares, Plaza de Santa Teresa, better known as **El Mercado Grande**, and **El Mercado Chico**. The former, situated outside the walls near the Alcázar Gate, takes its name from the large market which took place here, as opposed to the small one

*«El Mercado Chico» square. Town Hall.*

in the latter. El Mercado Grande was also the scene where town criers read out ordinances, and where the Inquisition held public hearings. Here, too, stood the corn exchange, as well as many taverns. The square was greatly reformed in the 16th century, when it was agreed that the porticoes should be made from carved stone and the spaces between measure 14 feet. Later, in the second half of the 19th century, the square was converted into a tree-lined garden with a bandstand, transferred to the Jardín del Recreo park in 1934, when the trees were also removed from «El Grande». A monument to La Santa now presides over the square, a popular meeting-point for locals and visitors alike.

El Mercado Chico, also a porticoed square, is the centre of official life in Avila, and it is here that we find the **Town Hall**. The building dates back to the 16th century, when the entire square was also altered. No longer used as a venue for dramatic performances and bullfights, a vegetable market continues to take place here every Friday, and the square is another popular meeting-place.

## Saint Teresa of Jesus

Head north out of the city of Ávila and follow the left bank of the Adaja River and you will come to the town of **Gotarrendura**, which lies at the start of the wide plain of La Moraña.

This town is closely linked to the life of St. Teresa and particularly to her childhood. Her parents owned a large estate of land and livestock, which they had inherited from Doña Teresa de las Cuevas, the saint's maternal grandmother.

The inhabitants of the village, who then numbered ninety-five, were witness to the important events in Saint Teresa's family. Her parents, Don Alonso Sánchez de Cepeda and Doña Beatriz de Ahumada, married in the autumn of 1509: the day was memorable for the whole village. The family spent many a long season here, for the harvest in summer and to escape the cold of Ávila in the winter. Everybody, especially Don Alonso, loved this relaxing place. In 1528 Doña Beatriz fell ill and died, and her body was taken to Ávila.

Over the years, almost all of Saint Teresa's brothers were to go to America and the estate was to be sold. The only thing now remaining from the Cepeda Ahumada country home is the base of a dovecote. According to traditional story, the stone from the house was used to build the existing parish church.

Saint Teresa was to call her convents «Palomaricos» after the «palomar» (dovecote) of her childhood home, where, in all simplicity and humility, glory is given to God.

*Gotarrendura: monument to Saint Teresa.*

*Gotarrendura: parish church.*

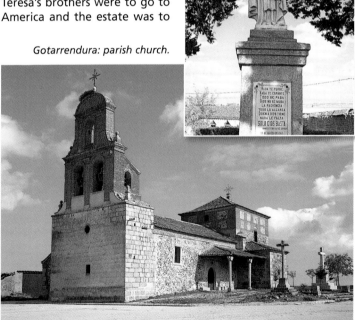

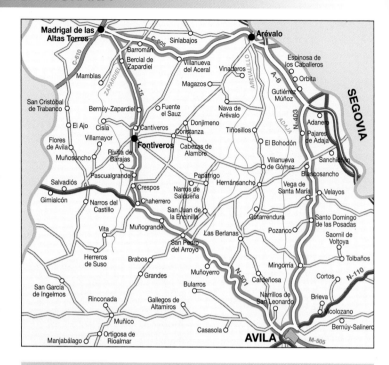

## 2. LA MORAÑA
Arévalo – Madrigal de las Altas Torres – Fontiveros

W̲e now head for the northern part of the province, comprising the different districts of **La Moraña** (meaning «Land of Moors») and **Arévalo.** The landscape now changes dramatically, with a predominance of rolling plains dedicated to the cultivation of cereals. We shall feel this change in all its aspects, particularly in the architecture. La Moraña has its own art, Mudéjar art, its origins lying in the scarcity of good stone, obliging buildings to be constructed of brick or adobe and mortar. We begin our route by leaving Ávila on the 403 road to the 6 railway, which will take us to Arévalo.

### ARÉVALO
Regional capital which lost all greater aspirations after the 16th century, becoming the present-day centre of the cereal trade. The historic centre of the city was declared Historic and Artistic Site of National Interest in 1970.

*La Moraña is characterized by its extensive cereal fields.*

## Fortifications and bridges

The city walls were built in the 12th century, though little now remains. The most important vestiges are the **Arco de la Cárcel,** with two pointed arches with rectangular *alfiz,* or moulding, and the **Arco de San Juan,** of which only a semi-hexagonal tower remains. Little, too remains, of the castle, restored some years ago. The castle received many important personages, including Blanca of Bourbon, the unhappy wife of Peter the Cruel, imprisoned here in 1353; Queen Isabel the Catholic, who lived here with her mother and brother until the age of ten; and the Duke of Osuna and the Prince of Orange, held prisoner here by King Philip IV.

Arévalo boasts four beautiful Mudéjar bridges. Over the Arevalillo, that of **Los Barros,** over

*View of Arévalo.*

*Arévalo: Arch of Medina.*

the Medina, that of **Llano** or **de Medina,** and over the Adaja, two: the **Puente de Valladolid** (in ruins) and that of **San Julián,** upstream and somewhat smaller.

## Church of Santa María la Mayor

Decorated on the outside with double arches, this church consists of a nave and apse. At the

*Arévalo Castle.*

*Church of Santa María la Mayor.*

foot of the church is a tower supported by an arch, terminating in a section of windows crowned by an element added in more modern times.

## Church of San Miguel

Another interesting example of Mudéjar art, with a doorway in the purest style. The sides are interesting due to the capricious

*Church of San Miguel.*

distribution and different shapes of the spaces.

Inside is an 18th-century altarpiece containing a series of 13 panels taken from an earlier altarpiece (15th century). These panels are attributed to an anonymous painter known as the «Maestro de Arévalo» and depict five scenes from the Passion, four from the legend of Saint Michael and four pairs of saints.

### Church of San Martín

The two towers of this church are the finest in Arévalo. They are known as the Tower of Los Ajedreces (in reference to the chessboard designs of the upper section), and the Torre Nueva.

### Church of San Juan Bautista

The most interesting feature of this church is its tower, unusually located on the right-hand side of the head, adjoining the city walls.

### Church of Santo Domingo

A late-15th century building with a fine grille closing the presbytery attributed to Laurencio de Ávila.

### Church of El Salvador

In 1562, Bernal Dávila and Luisa Briceño founded a chapel, known today as the Briceño Chapel, on the right-hand side of the building. This is the most interesting element in the church, presided as it is by an altarpiece by the sculptor Juan de Juni, completed by his son Isaac.

*Church of San Martín.*

*Church of El Salvador.*

### Church of Santiago, now San Nicolás Parish Church

Former Jesuits' college, founded by Hernán Tello de Guzmán, a knight of Saint James. Rebuilt according to baroque taste in the 17th century.

### Civil buildings

Arévalo also boasts a number of civil buildings manifesting the former wealth of the town. Outstanding are the palaces of the Marqués de los Altares in Calle de Santa María and the Marqués de Santa Marta, in the same street, with Renaissance doorway.

We now take the CL-605 road once more, to our next stop.

*Two views of Plaza del Arrabal.*

*Madrigal de las Altas Torres.*

## MADRIGAL DE LAS ALTAS TORRES

Important, age-old Castilian township whose importance began to grow in the 13th century after it was granted its own fueros (rights to collect taxes) and emancipation from Arévalo, on which it had formerly depended. John II frequently visited Madrigal, where he married and where his daughter,

*City wall towers.*

the future Queen Isabel the Catholic, was born in 1451.

## Fortifications

The walls of Madrigal, dating back to the late-13th century, are one of the finest existing examples of Mudéjar military architecture. The towers, unlike those of Ávila, are square and hollow and are surrounded by walls and moats.

We begin our tour at the **Puerta de Cantalapiedra,** featuring a large tower on one flank. Two more towers cross our path until we come to the much simpler **Arco de Medina.** The next entrance is the **Puerta de Arévalo,** formed by a huge tower whose base is the doorway. After admiring the best preserved stretch of wall, dotted with large towers, we come to the **Puerta de Peñaranda** or **Arco de los Caños,** of which little now remains. The remaining stretch to the Puerta de Cantalapiedra also contains several towers, all of them large in size, most notably the **Tower of El Rayo.**

## Church of Santa María del Castillo

A 12th-century Mudéjar church, rebuilt in the 18th century, which still conserves its original tower and heads.

*Church of Santa María del Castillo.*

*Church of San Nicolás.*

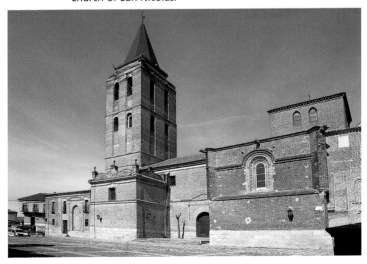

*Hospital de la Concepción.*

## Church of San Nicolás

One of the best conserved examples of the Mudéjar style, this church also features Renaissance additions which in no way alter the original construction. The exterior features are the apses and the magnificent tower, crowned by a slate spire and a weathercock, symbol of vigilance.

Notable in the interior are the magnificent Mudéjar roofs and structure. Two chapels were added in the 16th century, the so-called Capilla Dorada on the right and that founded by Francisco Ruiz de Medina, which has an interesting altarpiece with sculptures from the school of Berruguete.

*Palace of Juan II.*

Also outstanding is the alabaster tomb of Gonzalo Guiral on the left of the presbytery.

We cannot end our visit without admiring the Capilla Bautismal, where there is a small museum containing other interesting pieces from this church and other sources.

## Hospital de la Concepción

Founded in 1443 and rebuilt in the 16th century. Inside is the statue of Santo Cristo de las Injurias, an image much venerated in the region.

## Monastery of Nuestra Señora de Gracia

This monastery began to acquire importance when John II chose it as the last resting-place of Princess Catalina, who died in Madrigal in 1424. In 1499, the Catholic Queen con-fined two of her husband's illegitimate daughters, María of Aragon and María Esperanza of Aragon, here. The building, conserved practically intact, is one of the best examples of 15th-century noble houses. It was opened to the public as a museum on 8 September 1964 under the name of **Palace of Juan II** or the **Birth-place of Isabel the Catholic** (born here on 22 April 1451). Outstanding among the works on display here is a *Pietà* which, according to legend, was salvaged from the sea and donated to the monastery by the Catholic King.

## Convent of Augustine monks

The building formerly occupied by the nuns of Our Lady of Grace

*Queen Isabel the Catholic.*

*Convent of Agustine monks: tribute to Vasco de Quiroga.*

*Arco de Piedra, or the Stone Arch.*

1591, as Fray Luis de León died here on 23 August of that year. After the disentailment, the convent was stripped, and is now in ruins. Nevertheless, a fine courtyard in the purest Herreran style can be admired.

Madrigal also contains other interesting buildings, such as the **Arco de Piedra,** with its fine Plateresque front.

We now take road AV-P-115 to Fontiveros, the last stop on this route, before continuing the return journey to the city of Ávila.

## FONTIVEROS

### Parish church

With a length of 56 metres, this is the largest church on our route. The church was completed in two stages, as the nave and aisles are Mudéjar, dating back to the

became a masculine convent when the former moved to the Palacio de Juan II. It appears to have been completed around

*Fontiveros: parish church.*

*Saint John of the Cross.*

*Convent of Discalced Carmelites.*

12th century, whilst the late-Gothic head was added in the 16th century. Inside, the structures (remodelled in the 16th century) are notable. The outstanding chapel is the Capilla Real, devoted to John the Baptist and protected by a 16th-century grille.

## Convent of Discalced Carmelites

Founded in the paternal home of Saint John of the Cross, this convent has a 17th-century church with fine altarpieces by members of the Madrid school under the direction of Alonso Cano.

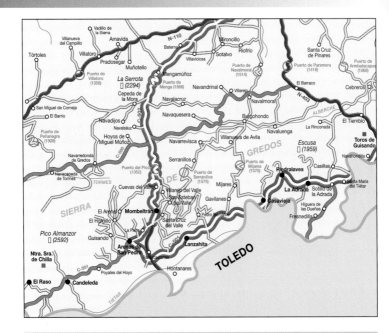

## 3. THE TIÉTAR VALLEY

Mombeltrán – Arenas de San Pedro – Toros de Guisando

*Barranco de las Cinco Villas (Gully of the five villages).*

In the south of the province, occupying the sun-soaked slopes of the Sierra de Gredos, this rich valley, marking the border with Toledo province, is watered by the River Tiétar. The valley's privileged situation has made it a popular destination in summer since the end of the last century.

Take National road 110 to the 502 to Arenas de San Pedro. Our first stop is Mombeltrán.

*Castle-Palace of Mombeltrán.*

## MOMBELTRÁN

Mombeltrán, along with the villages of Santa Cruz del Valle, Cuevas del Valle, Sant Esteban del Valle and Villarejo del Valle, make up the Barranco de las Cinco Villas, or the Mombeltrán Valley. One of the most interesting features of this district are the original construction methods used here, little changed since the 15th century. Houses have small fronts, large rears and no patio, with windows at the sides only and the bedrooms in the middle for protection against the cold. They have large projecting balconies which in the squares form archways supported by roughly-hewn wooden pillars with footings. Though our visit is chiefly concerned with Mombeltrán, other nearby villages also offer the chance to admire interesting works of art: **San Esteban,** with its late-15th-century Gothic church, featuring Plateresque

*Mombeltrán: Hospital de San Andrés.*

portal and a fine grille around the Capilla Mayor; **Villarejo,** which also boasts a 15th-century church, containing a fine statue of Saint Sebastian; and **Cuevas,** whose main feature is also a late-15th-century church, with four frontals of late-15th-century tiles from Talavera, and the remains of the Roman road, reaching as far as Puerto del Pico. Mombeltrán, formerly known as Colmenar de Arenas, changed its name when King Henry IV gave the place to his favourite, Beltrán de la Cueva.

## Castle-Palace
Ordered to be built in the mid-15th century by Beltrán de la Cueva, whose coat of arms is to be seen all over the building.

## Parish church
A 14th-century Gothic building

of great serenity and elegance. Notable Gothic and Plateresque grilles at the entrances to the chapels, and altars, adorned with tiles, dating back to the 16th and 17th centuries.

## Hospital de San Andrés
This ancient hospital for pilgrims was founded in 1517 by García Manso y Velasco and the front was adorned by a statue of Saint Andrew made of tiles, now lost. In 1797, Alfonso Regalado Rodríguez remodelled the inner courtyard, using brick as his principal material.

## ARENAS DE SAN PEDRO
An important township situated on the banks of the River Arenal and with a busy trade in timber, fruit, wine and oil. Its principal monuments include:

*View of Arenas de San Pedro.*

**Castle of the Sad Countess**

This Castillo de la Triste Condesa was built at the end of the 16th century as the residence of the Count of Castile, Ruy López de Avalos. The castle still conserves such original elements as its thick granite walls and the elegant inner windows with their strong Mudéjar influence.

*Castle of the Sad Countess.*

### Parish church

A 14th-century building, though the late-Gothic interior dates to the 15th. The outstanding exterior feature is the five-sectioned 16th-century tower, whilst the works of art exhibited in the interior include a Renaissance grille protecting the Chapel of the Tower and a monstrance made in around 1540 by one Alexo.

*Tower of the parish church of the Assumption.*

### Convent of San Pedro de Alcántara

Situated two kilometres from the village, this convent is hidden in the lovely pine and chestnut tree covered slopes of the Sierra de Gredos. It was Saint Peter of Alcántara himself who, in 1561, decided to found this community as his last resting-place.

The convent contains an interesting museum in which the Franciscan Order has gathered together a selection of works of sacred art, relics and testimonies to the faith of the founder.

*Chapel of San Pedro de Alcántara.*

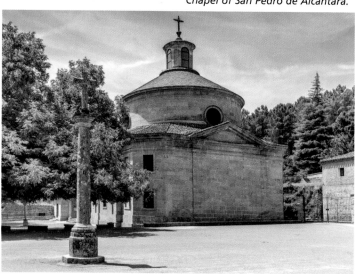

*Street of Arenas de San Pedro.*

## Palace of Prince Luis

This site was chosen by the prince, brother of Charles III to install his cultured, refined court. The palace features an impressive front, entirely in granite, and a lovely staircase inspired by that in the Royal Palace, Madrid.

*El Águila Caves.*

### El Águila Caves

Taking the road from Ramacastañas, we reach the famous El Águila Caves. Discovered early this century, these are huge subterranean spaces inhabited by stalactites and stalagmites.

### FROM CANDELEDA TO PEDRO BERNARDO

Though we are heading for Lanzahita along the CL-501 road, we should stop off at **Candeleda,** on the limits of the province, with its 15th-century Gothic church and the charming **Sanc-**

*Candeleda and the Siera de Gredos.*

*Candeleda: Sanctuary of Nuestra Señor de Chilla.*

*Lanzahita: parish church.*

tuary of **Nuestra Señor de Chilla,** built in the 18th century, the religious centre of the valley. Another important visit is the archaeological site of **El Raso,** dating back to around the 4th century BC.

We now continue along the CL-501 road towards Madrid. Our first stop is **Lanzahita,** with an interesting early-16th-century church. Next are **Casavieja, Piedralaves**, **La Adrada** and **Pedro Bernardo,** which still con-

*La Eliza gorge, in the surroundings of Lanzahíta.*

*Piedralaves.*

serves the ruins of the castle built by Ruy López de Avalos and a large parish church dating from the mid-16th century. At the crossroads of the Sotillo de la Adrada with San Martín de Valdeiglesias roads, we take the direction of Toros de Guisando, the last stop on this route.

## Toros de Guisando

On the hill of the same name in the dying foothills of the Sierra de Gredos is a group of four stone sculptures representing *verracos,* or sculptures of bulls and pigs. These date back to the 2nd century BC and bear Iberian and Latin inscriptions. The exact meaning

*La Adrada Castle.*

*View of Pedro Bernardo.*

*Toros de Guisando.*

of these manifestations of Celtic culture are not known, though it is thought by many that they were made to protect the fields and cattle.

This spot is also famous because it was here that Henry IV of Castile and his sister Isabel reached the Concord of Toros de Guisando in 1468, putting an end to the Castilian Civil War.

*Street of Guisando.*

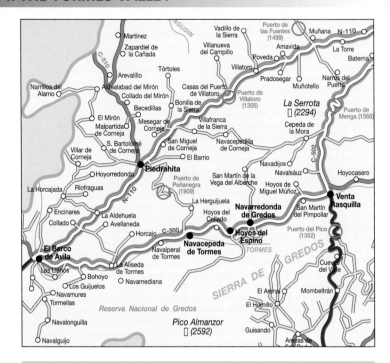

## 4. THE TORMES VALLEY
El Barco de Ávila – Piedrahita.

The beauty of the district we shall now visit resides in its scenery. Our route is a continuous invitation to pause and admire the beauty of one of the most attractive landscapes on the Iberian Peninsula. This is the Sierra de Gredos, over one hundred kilometres of soaring mountain peaks, including El Pico Almanzor (2,592 metres), Las Cinco Lagunas, El Circo de Gredos and La Laguna.

We leave Ávila on the N-110 road, taking the N-502 to **Venta Rasquilla,** then the AV-941 towards **El Barco de Ávila,** slowly beginning to discovery the landscape, becoming gradually enchanted by its natural beauty. All the villages we shall visit have grown up around their little parish churches, crowned by spire or tower. The houses are built of stone and have large doors with posts and lintels tied to the wall by strong palisades.

We shall begin with the **Parador de Turismo de Gredos, Navarredonda de Gredos,** with its interesting church, **Hoyos del Es-**

*Laguna Grande, Sierra de Gredos.*

**pino** and **Navacepeda de Tormes,** where we can admire the «Puente de las Paredes», under which run the clean, pure wa-

*Sierra de Gredos.*

*Young deer in the surroundings of Hoyos del Espino.*

ters of the Sierra. In **Navalperal de Tormes,** we shall visit the main square, finally arriving at El Barco de Ávila, an absolutely essential visit.

## EL BARCO DE ÁVILA

An important communications point, dominating the routes between Castile and Andalusia. For this reason, ruined walls can still

*The city walls at El Barco de Ávila. Ávila Gate.*

*Roman bridge on the River Tormes at El Barco de Ávila.*

be seen here, as well as an interesting main square with porticoes and noble houses.

## Walls

Built from rough stone, these are almost two metres thick and are reinforced by square towers. Of the gates, only the «Puerta de Ávila», of great simplicity, survives.

## Castle-Palace of the Dukes of Alba

The remains of this old fortress dominate the village. It belonged to the House of Alba, former lords of the Valdecorneja and, after being abandoned, was converted into a cemetery. Little remains of the interior, except the marks of the different storeys. Part of the arcades of its courtyard are now in the Plaza Mayor.

## Roman Bridge

A monumental, 125 metre long monumental bridge crossing the Tormes, with seven unequal arches, two of them pointed and the others semicircular.

## Parish church

Built in the 14th century, the interior is very simple, covered with Gothic vaults, their keys decorated with coats of arms of the House of Alba or such motifs as the keys of Saint Peter, a boat, a vase of lilies and two crossed pairs of compasses. The church also contains good 15th-century grilles attributed to Juan de Ávila, a disciple of Juan Francés.

The museum installed in the antesacristy, the sacristy and two other dependencies above, communicated with the ground floor by a 16th-century Gothic staircase,

*El Barco de Ávila: Parish church of Nuestra Señora de la Asunción.*

has an interesting collection of sacred art, including two anonymous 15th-century panels representing *Christ in the Temple* and *The Death of the Virgin.*

We now take the N-110 road towards Ávila, until we reach Piedrahita.

*Piedrahíta: parish church.*

## PIEDRAHÍTA

Capital of the Corneja Valley, Piedrahíta was given by Henry II to García Alvarez de Toledo, in 1472 made Duke of Alba.

### Parish church

This church is thought to have been founded in the 13th century by Queen Berenguela, wife of Alphonse IX. Little remains of the original building, due to the many reforms which took place in the 16th and 18th centuries. Outstanding is the lovely south door, in Renaissance style, with interesting floral decoration and a statue of the Virgin.

The interior features the altarpiece over the Altar of the Kings, in the south aisle, presided over by an image of the Virgin with the Child in Her Arms (early-

*Piedrahíta: Town Hall and Palace of the Dukes of Alba.*

15th century). There is also a fine Gothic grille in the Chapel of Los Tamayo, and two 17th-century wrought iron eagles for lecterns.

## Convent of Calced Carmelites

Among the works displayed here is a *Christ of the Patience*, perhaps by the school of Alonso Cano, kept in the choir.

## Former Convent of Dominicans

Founded by the dukes of Alba and built in the late-14th century, according to the inscription on a stone in the chapel.

## Palace of the Dukes of Alba

Built by the French architect Jaime Marquet between 1755 and 1766, this palace is in early Neo-Classical style.

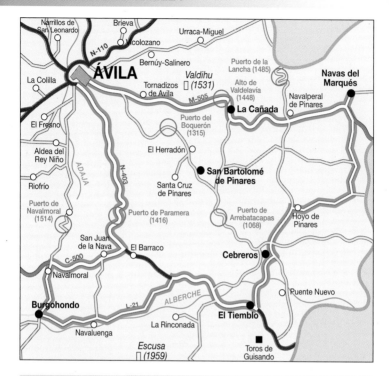

## 5. THE ALBERCHE VALLEY
Las Navas del Marqués – Cebreros – El Tiemblo – Burgohondo

This zone lies in the east of Ávila province and includes the Alberche Valley and the Pinares district. Due to its mild climate and proximity to Madrid, many people have installed their second residence in this region. This small zone contains the sierras of Paramera, Cuerda de los Polvisos and Malagón which, along with the foothills of the Sierra de Gredos, form a deep valley along which runs the River Alberche. Once more, the landscape is the main source of wealth here.

We begin our tour by taking the CL-505 road towards San Lorenzo de El Escorial, coming to our first stop, Las Navas del Marqués.

### LAS NAVAS DEL MARQUÉS
A small town which has become an important summer resort thanks to its good road and rail communications with Madrid. Its name refers to the fact that the town once belonged to the Marquis of Las Navas, Pedro de Ávila, as it was formerly known as

*Navalmoral pass.*

*Alberche Valley landscape.*

Las Navas de Pinares. Before beginning our visit we can take the local road to **Peguerinos,** admiring the impressive scenery.

## Parish church

A church with a nave and two aisles separated by pointed arches supported by Doric columns decorated with the heraldic motifs of Pedro de Ávila, patron of the church. The head of the church is particularly impressive, dating back to the 16th century, with Gothic vault and an interesting painting of Saint Blas.

## Convent of San Pablo

Convent founded by Pedro de Ávila, first Marquis of Las Navas, in

*Las Navas del Marqués: the Parish church and Convent of San Pablo..*

1547. Impressive large granite church.

### Magalia Castle

Built by the first Marquis of Las Navas in the mid-16th century, this palace has a lovely square court-yard with arches over Ionic columns on the first floor and an architrave over Doric columns on the second.

As with most of the fortress-palaces of this period, the palace has a square groundplan with towers at the corners and is con-structed in stone from Berrueco. Pedro de Ávila's love of classical Antiquity led him to collect Ro-man inscriptions from Mérida, which he then set into the walls of the entrance, courtyard and principal dependencies of the palace.

### CEBREROS

We now retrace our steps to Navalperal de Pinares to take

*Las Navas del Marqués: Magalia Castle.*

*Overall view of Cebreros.*

local road AV-502 to El Hoyo de Pinares and then Cebreros. Those with time to spare can stop in **Cañada** instead of in Navalperal, taking the road which also leads to Cebreros, but via **San Bartolomé de Pinares,** admiring the scenery and visiting the church with its large late-16th-century altarpiece, and the **Puerto de Arrebatacapas.** This alternative route allows the visitor to fully appreciate the changing landscape as we enter the Alberche Valley and pause in Cebreros.

## Old church

This is a 14th-century building with a fine front emblazoned with the coat of arms of Francisco de la Fuente, bishop of Ávila.
Its nave and aisles, separated by semicircular arches decorated with globes, date back to the 15th century.

## Parish church

Popular tradition compares this church with the Monastery of San Lorenzo de El Escorial, even affirming that its author was Juan de Herrera. However, this belief does not bear out in reality, as the church appears to date from around 1560.
The interior contains a fine main altarpiece with paintings by

*Cebreros: the old church.*

*El Tiemblo: Chapel of San Antonio.*

Jusepe Leonardo of Madrid, and sculptures by a follower of Alonso Cano. The sides feature two more altarpieces imitating the style of the first.

## EL TIEMBLO

We now take the same road towards national road 403 to El Tiemblo, with its interesting church and town hall, then con-

*El Burguillo Reservoir.*

*Burgohondo: Abbey of Santa María de la Asunción.*

tinuing towards Ávila along local road AV-902, when we begin to glimpse the Alberche Valley.

## BURGOHONDO

Village declared a historic and artistic monument in 1983. Charming streets and interesting parish church, formerly an Augustine abbey.

## Abbey of Santa María

The earliest records of the foundation of this church date to 1178 in a bull mentioning the abbey as *Monasterium S(an)c(t)e Marie de Fundo*. Later documents specify that it belonged to the Order of Saint Augustine, referring to the monastery as *Burgo de Fondo*. What is certain is that this area of the province was repopulated after the Reconquest thanks to the presence of this religious foundation, which levelled land and opened up terrain for cultivation, bringing with it many farm labourers and shepherds, forming as many as thirteen villages tied to the monastery.

The foundation reached its maximum splendour in the 16th century, when it even had criminal jurisdiction. Decline began to set in during the 18th century, until in 1795 the monastery was finally closed and converted into a parish church on the orders of the chapter of Ávila Cathedral. The 12th century church is Romanesque in style, its roofs dating back to the 16th century. The nave is Mudéjar, bevelled at either end.

From Burgohondo, we take local road AV-900 to national road N-403, which will take us back to the city of Ávila.